DEDICAT

To those who have loved fiercely and lost painfully, yet refuse to give up on love.

To the ones who have mistaken illusions for truth but found the strength to see clearly.

This book is for the hearts that crave something real—love that doesn't hide behind masks.

May these pages help you break free from deception and embrace relationships built on honesty.

Above all, may you always choose love that is transparent, loyal, and true.

TABLE OF CONTENTS

LOYALTY AND LOVE IS TRANSPARENT

VINCENT RYAN

INTRODUCTION

I read somewhere that relationships are delicate ecosystems where emotions, trust, and personal histories intertwine. At their best, they offer companionship, security, and a sense of belonging. At their worst, they become battlegrounds of unspoken resentments, manipulations, and emotional exhaustion. Some relationships thrive, blossoming into lifelong partnerships built on honesty, mutual respect, and genuine effort. Others, however, slowly unravel, revealing painful truths that were once hidden beneath layers of attraction and hope.

This book is a deep dive into the complexities of human relationships—why they succeed, why they fail, and the illusions that keep us trapped in unhealthy cycles. It is an exploration of both the beauty and the brutality of love, revealing the red flags we often ignore, the silent struggles that erode trust, and the false hopes that lead us astray. Through personal experiences, observations, and hard-earned wisdom, I aim to strip away the romanticized versions of love we are fed and expose the reality of what it takes to build something real.

I have witnessed and experienced the highs and lows of love. I have seen people fall for charming illusions, only to wake up in nightmares. I have seen partners who appeared devoted but were merely skilled in deception. I have also seen relationships that defied the odds—ones that, through honesty, patience, and intentional effort, grew into powerful, unshakable bonds. These experiences have shaped my understanding of love, trust, and what it truly means to be loyal.

Within these pages, you will find stories of deception—partners who wore masks, relationships poisoned by manipulation, and love that was conditional rather than unconditional. You will also find lessons on resilience, on choosing love with clarity rather than desperation, and on recognizing the difference between affection and control. This book does not promise a universal formula for love, nor does it pretend to have all the answers. Instead, it offers perspectives, lessons, and, most importantly, a mirror for self-reflection.

Whether you are searching for love, healing from past wounds, or strengthening a current relationship, my hope is that these pages will provide clarity and wisdom. Love should not be a puzzle that leaves you questioning your worth. It should be a transparent space where loyalty is not a demand but a natural outcome of mutual respect, understanding, and effort.

Let's begin this journey together—one where love is no longer a game of illusions but a path to something real, something honest, and something that truly lasts.

CHAPTER ONE

THE ILLUSION OF LOVE

Many relationships start with charm. Some people are skilled at creating a version of themselves that is desirable, saying all the right words, and doing all the right things. In the excitement of new love, it's easy to overlook inconsistencies, brush off small lies, or excuse behaviors that later become significant issues.

I used to believe that love was enough to hold a relationship together. That as long as two people loved each other, they could overcome anything. It was a comforting idea, the kind of belief that made me stay in relationships longer than I should have, hoping that love alone would fix the cracks that were already too deep.

But love—at least the way many of us imagine it—is an illusion.

Some illusions go beyond charm and enter dangerous territories. A privileged attitude can make a partner feel entitled to control and compulsive lying can turn a relationship into an emotional maze.

I learned this the hard way.

Illusions in love don't last forever, but recognizing them early can prevent unnecessary heartbreak. Some warning signs include:

- **Too much, too soon** – If someone rushes intimacy or commitment, they may be trying to create an illusion rather than build something real.
- **Inconsistencies in stories** – If a partner's past keeps changing or they contradict themselves often, they may not be as transparent as they seem.
- **Defensiveness when questioned** – Someone who becomes protective and guarded, reacts aggressively to simple questions may be hiding something.
- **Lack of accountability** – If they always blame others for their past failures and find it hard to/never admit wrongdoing, it may be a pattern.

The truth is, love—real love—isn't just about emotions. It's about consistency, effort, and a willingness to grow together. And sometimes, the hardest but most important thing to do is let go of the illusion and make room for something real.

Some lies are small, seemingly harmless. Others are grand, orchestrated with precision to create a false sense of security. But no matter the size, deception carries weight, and sooner or later, it becomes unbearable.

Some people enter relationships to seek validation, control, or personal advantage. They curate a version of themselves that suits their partner's desires, not because they genuinely share those values, but because it gives them access to what they want.

Let's say you meet someone at a book club and you're drawn to their intelligence. They speak passionately about honesty, commitment, and emotional maturity. They reassure you that they were done with games and wanted something real but what you don't know is that they had studied you, delicately molding themselves into the person you want. When you express insecurities, they comfort you, not out of care, but to maintain their image as the "perfect" person. Over time, their interest fades, but instead of leaving, they string you along, keeping you emotionally invested while seeking validation from other people.

By the time you realize that you had been in love with an illusion, the betrayal wouldn't just be about cheating—it would sum up to the months invested which will make you question every moment you shared.

Deception in relationships doesn't necessarily start with ill intent. Sometimes, people lie to avoid conflict, protect their image, or because they are afraid of losing their partner. But no matter the reason, every lie chips away at trust.

Staying with a partner who continually lies, even if it's just small things, will start to create a doubt for you. If a big issue arises, you won't be certain if they're being honest with you or not and that's where this behavior really becomes a major problem. Even if they've done nothing wrong, they've given you many reasons not to trust them.

Not all deception is verbal. Some partners manipulate through actions, silence, or emotional games designed to keep the other person uncertain.

I vaguely remember a situation with a young woman whose story sounded all too familiar—claiming she could do whatever she wanted. Before anything even happened between us, I was upfront about my past experiences and asked her to be honest with me. So, I asked, "*Are you really single, or are you just playing games*?"

After a moment, she admitted that she had a boyfriend, but things were complicated. Instead of going any further, I offered her some relationship advice, telling her that we didn't have to do this. She agreed, and I left.

The next day, I got an unexpected call—from her boyfriend. To my surprise, he wasn't aggressive or disrespectful. Instead, he was just a man looking for answers. He expressed his concerns about her cheating and wanted to know the extent of my involvement with her. I spoke to him honestly, assuring him that nothing had happened between us.

He then asked me—respectfully—to stop contacting her, explaining that they were going through a rough patch and trying to work things out. Before we ended the call, I mentioned that she had said she truly loved him and wished he would open up and communicate better. He sighed and admitted, "*Yeah, I know… I need to fix that*". Before hanging up, he simply said, *Peace*.

After experiencing so many toxic situations, I had made it a point to give women a way out—encouraging them to communicate, compromise, and work on their relationships. Unfortunately, most felt it was a lost cause. But in this case, I left knowing I had helped save at least one relationship, and that, to me, was a win.

Manipulation is not necessarily harmful when it is used to avoid turmoil in a relationship but it can turn dark and become exploitation, the use of deception to mold and control another's response for the benefit of the manipulator. This can lead to problems with intimacy, trust, respect and security to mention a few.

Deception in relationships often follow a pattern. While every situation is unique, common signs include inconsistencies, deflection, gaslighting, secrecy to mention a few.

Loyalty and love should never require deception. It makes one question their judgment, their memories, and sometimes even their self-worth. The question to always ask is: If honesty is uncomfortable for them, can I ever truly feel safe with them?

CHAPTER TWO

THE ILLUSION OF PASSION AND PERFECTION

We all want the perfect relationship. The perfect partner. The kind of love that feels written in the stars. A love where there are no doubts, no complications, just two people who fit seamlessly together. We believe that when the right person comes along, everything will just click.

But passion, on its own, and perfection, in itself, are illusions.

I've been in relationships where passion burned so brightly that nothing else seemed to matter. The chemistry was undeniable, the attraction magnetic. In those moments, I convinced myself that passion meant love—that if we felt this strongly, nothing else mattered. But I was wrong.

Passion, without stability, is chaos. When we confuse infatuation for compatibility, mistake sexual chemistry for emotional depth, we build relationships on a foundation of sand and by the time we realize the cracks in the illusion, we are already too deep.

The same applies to perfection. We've been conditioned to chase an ideal—a flawless partner, a picture-perfect relationship. But this pursuit only leads to disappointment. Perfection is not love. It's a fantasy that blinds us to the beauty of what's real.

We know passion pulls us into a world where emotions run high and every touch and glance feels electric. It's the kind of love that makes you lose yourself in the moment but the problem with passion is that it isn't meant to be the foundation of a relationship. Passion fades. It always does. And when it does, we're left with what truly matters—compatibility, emotional safety, and shared values. Yet, many people chase the feeling of passion rather than the substance of a real relationship. They believe that if the spark fades, the relationship is failing. They mistake emotional highs and lows for depth. They equate instability with excitement, confusing emotional turbulence with love.

When we are deeply drawn to someone, we become blind to warning signs. We start making excuses for things that should never be ignored. "They're just jealous because they love me so much", "They get angry because they're passionate."

But none of this is love. Love doesn't thrive in toxicity. Passion makes dysfunction seem romantic. It tricks people into believing that emotional chaos is proof of love. In reality, it's just emotional addiction.

I've seen it too many times—people staying in unhealthy relationships simply because they don't want to lose the feeling. They confuse their attachment with love when, in reality, they're just addicted to the emotional rush.

True love shouldn't be about constant adrenaline. It should be about knowing someone is truly for you—without fear, without doubt, without instability.

We live in a world obsessed with perfection. Movies, books, and social media have sold us a vision of love that is effortless, and magical. We see highlight reels of happy couples and assume that's how love should be but behind every perfect Instagram post is real effort, struggle, and compromise. The truth is, no relationship is effortless. No partner is flawless and expecting otherwise only sets us up for disappointment.

When people chase both passion and perfection, they set themselves up for heartbreak. They expect love to be an all-consuming force that is thrilling and flawless. But passion, as powerful as it is, does not equal compatibility. And perfection, as desirable as it seems, does not exist. The result equates to relationships that are either:

1. Too intense but lacking stability: When a relationship is built solely on passion, it lacks the foundation to endure real-life challenges. The highs are exhilarating, but the lows are devastating. Arguments become explosive, misunderstandings escalate quickly, and without emotional security, the relationship becomes a rollercoaster ride of temporary bliss

and inevitable disappointment. True love isn't just about intensity; it's about consistency, trust, and the ability to weather storms together.

2. Too idealized but emotionally empty: The idea of a "perfect" relationship is often based on external qualities—having a partner who looks good on paper, meets all the societal checkboxes, or aligns with an unrealistic fantasy. But perfection without emotional depth leads to an empty partnership. There's no vulnerability, no real connection—just a performance of love rather than the experience of it. A relationship built on perfectionism forces both partners to suppress their true selves, creating an environment where honesty and emotional safety are sacrificed for the sake of maintaining an illusion. True intimacy comes from embracing imperfections, not avoiding them.

Since we've established that chasing passion and perfection alone is dangerous, here are some ways it sabotages real love:

1. We Overlook Great Partners: Many people convince themselves, "I'll know it's right when it's perfect," only to spend their lives searching for something that doesn't exist. Thereby, missing out on truly wonderful relationships because the person doesn't match their ideal.
2. We Become Dissatisfied with Reality: When we expect perfection, we focus on what's missing instead of what's

there. We obsess over flaws, believing that love should never feel difficult.

3. We Chase an Unattainable Fantasy: Some people are constantly searching for "the one" who will meet every expectation. They jump from relationship to relationship, always leaving when reality doesn't match their idealized vision.

True love isn't found in the thrill of the chase or in a perfect fantasy. It's built through trust, patience, and the willingness to embrace imperfection.

CHAPTER THREE

THE ILLUSION OF CHEMISTRY AND DESTINY

Both destiny and chemistry can be intoxicating illusions, promising something that feels fated or perfect. But as I've learned through my own experiences, these illusions can cloud our judgment. They create an expectation of effortless love and compatibility, which ultimately isn't sustainable. Real relationships, the ones that stand the test of time, are built on conscious effort, emotional growth, and mutual respect.

We often hear that "everything happens for a reason," or that "people are meant to be." These phrases have the power to comfort, to provide solace when faced with uncertainty, but they also carry the weight of an illusion. The belief in destiny, in a fate that brings two people together, creates a narrative that can shape our expectations and cloud our judgment. It's easy to get swept up in the idea that life is leading you down a preordained path, and the people you meet along the way are there for a reason.

But is it destiny that brings us together? Or is it simply chance, circumstance, and timing?

I've been there, standing across from someone, feeling an unexplainable pull. It was as though the universe had orchestrated our meeting, that we were supposed to cross paths in that exact moment. I remember thinking that this person was "the one," that we were destined to build something beautiful. In hindsight, it was a series of coincidences, no different from the countless people I've met in my life. What I mistook for destiny was nothing more than a fleeting connection.

Chemistry is the spark we feel when we meet someone and everything seems to click—like we've known them forever. It's the undeniable connection, the electric energy that makes your heart race. It's the butterflies in your stomach, the excited anticipation of seeing someone again. Chemistry is thrilling, and when you experience it, it feels like magic but chemistry is not always a sign of something deeper, something long-lasting. Chemistry, while real, can often be mistaken for compatibility. We get swept away by the intensity of attraction and convince ourselves that this is the person we're meant to be with. We mistake the high of chemistry for the foundation of a lasting relationship.

The problem with all these is that it can make us blind to the reality of a relationship. We might think that love will come easily because it's "meant to be," then we forget that relationships take work, require understanding, patience, effort—qualities that can't be fulfilled by destiny alone. I've experienced that "instant spark," that feeling of knowing someone is right for you even before you've gotten to know them. It's easy to think that this kind of connection is proof of something deeper, something destined. But as time goes on, the intensity fades, and what you're left with is the reality of who the person truly is—and whether or not you actually share values, goals, and a mutual understanding.

And so I ask, what happens when the chemistry fades?

That initial excitement and intensity—filled with passionate glances and spontaneous adventures—begins to diminish over time. And while chemistry is important, it's not the glue that holds a relationship together. Without a solid foundation built on shared values and open communication, the relationship starts to unravel.

I've seen relationships where, once the initial thrill subsides, partners are left wondering what really sustains their bond. If you don't share the same core beliefs or if you haven't invested in deep, honest conversations, there's nothing to lean on when challenges arise. It's like constructing a house with flashy, modern decor but with a weak foundation—eventually, the structure crumbles under pressure.

Without shared values, conflicts become harder to resolve because you're essentially speaking different languages when it comes to priorities, ethics, and life goals. And when communication is poor, misunderstandings grow. You might have moments where you feel a brief resurgence of attraction, but they quickly give way to the reality that the relationship lacks depth. In the end, the chemistry alone isn't enough to carry a partnership through the inevitable ups and downs of life. The relationship crumbles because there's no lasting substance to support it—a support system that only real connection, mutual respect, and consistent dialogue can provide.

Again, without the foundation of shared values and communication, the relationship crumbles. It's easy to be addicted to the rush of chemistry, but real love is more than just those fleeting moments. Chemistry might bring people together, but it's the compatibility and emotional connection that keeps them there.

When I reflect on my past relationships, I realize that I often fell for the illusion of destiny and chemistry—blinded by the excitement of the moment, believing that they were signs of something deeper. In the end, I had to learn the hard way that love isn't built on these illusions. It's built on the foundation of choosing each other every day, and on the understanding that love isn't always instant—it's a process, one that grows stronger with time and commitment.

In the end, relationships don't thrive on destiny. They thrive on conscious choices and mutual respect. That's the part we often forget when we get caught up in the illusion. And chemistry, like destiny, is just the beginning. It's what comes after—the commitment to understanding, growing, and compromising—that determines whether a relationship will last.

So next time you feel that spark or think that fate has brought you together, pause. Ask yourself if it's real chemistry or just the rush of infatuation. Ask yourself if it's truly destiny, or just the timing and circumstances aligning for a moment. The real test of love comes after the chemistry fades, when the fairy tale is over, and reality sets in. That's when the true depth of the relationship is revealed.

CHAPTER FOUR

THE ILLUSION OF HAPPINESS AND INDEPENDENCE

In our world where independence is associated with strength, and happiness is seen as something we must chase relentlessly, we are often told that true happiness comes from within and that we should be whole on our own before committing to someone else but while there is some truth in this, the modern narrative has changed the meaning of happiness and independence in relationships.

The hard truth is no relationship can thrive on complete independence, and no person is an island. The idea that we can be perfectly happy and self-sufficient, with or without a partner, is an illusion that creates unrealistic expectations, leading to emotional detachment and an unwillingness to be vulnerable. As we go further, I will break down how this illusion forms, why it's dangerous, and how it can sabotage both romantic relationships and personal fulfillment.

Social media is filled with posts about not needing anyone, focusing on self, and prioritizing personal goals over relationships. While there is nothing wrong with self-growth, this message defeats the beauty of interdependence, mutual support and shared growth.

Some enforcers of this idea could be fear of vulnerability, trauma from past relationships and more. The result? Many people enter relationships with the belief that they don't need anyone, only to find themselves emotionally disconnected and struggling with intimacy.

HOW THIS COULD MANIFEST IN RELATIONSHIPS

1. Avoiding Emotional Dependence - Some individuals pride themselves on not relying on their partner for emotional support. I've seen individuals actively convincing themselves that expressing needs is burdensome, which is quite appalling because it is general knowledge that over time, this creates distance in the relationship, as their partner feels unneeded or unwanted.
2. Refusing to Compromise - A relationship requires flexibility, but when one or both partners are too focused on maintaining their independence, they resist making sacrifices. There's this fear that compromising means losing their sense of self, when in reality, healthy compromise strengthens a relationship.
3. Prioritizing the Self Over the Relationship - Though self-care and individuality are essential, some people take it to an extreme—putting their wants, needs, and aspirations far above their partner's. This can make the relationship feel one-sided, where one person is always accommodating while the other remains self-focused.
4. Fear of Commitment - Some individuals use independence as a shield to avoid deep commitment. They enjoy

companionship but hesitate to merge their lives with someone else, fearing it will strip them of their autonomy.

We could argue that these highlighted issues need to be tackled individually but this just proves my point on the craze of self sufficiency. We need to accept that we cannot always handle it on our own, then we can move on.

"Are you truly happy?" is a question I find that exposes lots of these issues but is rarely asked. Happiness has been turned into a performance. Many adopt the "fake it till you make it" approach, believing that if they act happy long enough, it will eventually become real. Newsflash, forcing happiness cannot equate to true contentment. Many people in modern relationships suppress their emotional struggles, convincing themselves that if they just focus on themselves, they will be happy. They distract themselves with career achievements, vacations, or casual dating—anything to avoid confronting the fact that they feel empty inside.

Another angle, many people mistake comfort for happiness. If a relationship is easy and non-confrontational, they assume they are happy. But I can't stress enough on the fact that true happiness in a relationship comes from emotional fulfillment, not just the absence of arguments or drama. Here are some questions to ask yourself:

- Are you truly happy, or are you just avoiding loneliness?
- Do you feel emotionally connected, or just entertained?

- Are you growing with your partner, or are you stagnant together?

When people force themselves to believe they are happy in a relationship, they are essentially living in denial—convincing themselves that their dissatisfaction is temporary, that their unspoken frustrations aren't serious, or that love means enduring discomfort in silence. They cling to the illusion of happiness, telling themselves that things will improve or that their emotions are just overreactions. But in reality, suppressing emotions doesn't make them disappear; it only buries them deeper, where they grow into something far more destructive.

At first, this suppression might seem like a form of compromise—choosing peace over confrontation. But over time, the weight of unexpressed emotions accumulates, leading to resentment. Every need not yet met, every ignored concern, and every moment of dishonesty with oneself becomes a quiet grievance. It may start with small things—laughing off a dismissive comment, swallowing frustration when a partner is emotionally unavailable, or pretending not to care when boundaries are crossed. But these unresolved feelings don't stay hidden forever. They simmer beneath the surface, creating a growing emotional distance.

Emotional exhaustion soon follows. Constantly pretending to be happy is draining. It takes an immense amount of energy to suppress feelings of disappointment, frustration, or loneliness. People in this state may begin to feel numb, disconnected, or trapped in a cycle of self-doubt, wondering if their dissatisfaction is valid or if they're simply being ungrateful. They might even gaslight themselves into believing they should be happy because their relationship "looks good" on paper.

And then, the inevitable happens—a sudden emotional breakdown. Whether it's an explosive argument, an unexpected emotional outburst, or an abrupt decision to leave, the weight of suppression becomes unbearable. The person who has spent so long pretending everything is fine eventually reaches their breaking point. What could have been addressed in smaller conversations becomes a crisis, leading to decisions made in anger or exhaustion rather than clarity and understanding.

True happiness in a relationship isn't about forcing positivity or avoiding difficult conversations. It comes from honesty, emotional safety, and the ability to express feelings without fear. Pretending to be happy may offer temporary comfort, but in the long run, it only creates deeper wounds that are much harder to heal.

5 SUGGESTIONS ON HOW TO BREAK FREE FROM THIS ILLUSION

1. Redefine Independence in Relationships: I strongly believe that independence should not mean emotional isolation. It's okay to need your partner. Emotional reliance does not mean dependency—it means trust.

2. Embrace Vulnerability: The fear of vulnerability keeps people stuck in this illusion. Real intimacy requires opening up, even if it feels uncomfortable.
3. Differentiate Real Happiness from Superficial Joy: Reflect on whether your joy is genuine or just a performance. Ask yourself, do I hide parts of myself, am I emotionally safe, do I feel fulfilled when I'm with my partner.. etc.
4. Let Go of the "I Don't Need Anyone" Mindset: Let's chorus this together: "relationships thrive on mutual support". No one is truly independent—humans are wired for connection. The key is balance: maintaining individuality while allowing someone else to be an integral part of your life.
5. Seek True Happiness, Not the Illusion of It: This means you need to have deep, meaningful conversations with your partner, address issues instead of ignoring them and find joy in emotional connection rather than just surface-level excitement.

True happiness in a relationship doesn't come from proving you can be fine on your own. It comes from the security of knowing you have someone to share your life with. Likewise, independence does not mean refusing to rely on a partner—it means maintaining your sense of self while also allowing your relationship to flourish.

And happiness is real when it is shared—not when it is performed

CHAPTER FIVE

THE ILLUSION OF VALIDATION

It feels good to be seen, to be appreciated, to be wanted. Many of us enter relationships believing that our partner's approval will be the key to our happiness. We think that if someone loves us enough, compliments us enough, or chooses us above all else, then we'll finally feel secure within ourselves. But that belief is an illusion.

Validation from a partner can be comforting, but it is not a foundation for love. A relationship built on the need for external reassurance is like a house of cards—fragile, dependent on constant reinforcement, and easily collapsible, the moment that validation is withdrawn. True confidence and security in love do not come from being desired but from knowing our own worth.

I've been in relationships where I mistook validation for love. The constant praise, the reassurance, the way my partner's admiration made me feel like I was finally enough. It was intoxicating. But the problem with relying on someone else to affirm your worth is that their validation becomes a necessity rather than a bonus. When they withdraw it—whether intentionally or simply because they are dealing with their own struggles—your sense of security crumbles.

Validation initially feels like reassurance, like proof that we are worthy, desirable, and valued. When we receive it from a partner—whether through words of affirmation, attention, or affection—it reinforces our sense of self-worth. But when we become too reliant on external validation, it turns into an emotional trap. Instead of feeling secure in ourselves, we become dependent on another person's perception of us. Their approval becomes the measure of our worth, and without it, we feel lost, anxious, or even invisible.

The need for validation which often leads to emotional dependency because it creates a cycle where self-worth is tied to external approval usually happens in this manner:

1. Seeking Constant Reassurance: When someone craves validation, they rely on their partner to affirm their worth, attractiveness, intelligence, or importance. This constant need for reassurance prevents them from developing a solid sense of self. Over time, they start depending on their food partner's approval to feel secure, making them emotionally fragile when that approval isn't readily given.
2. Fear of Being Alone: People who seek validation often equate love with attention. When they don't receive it, they feel unloved or abandoned. This fear makes them tolerate unhealthy dynamics, stay in toxic relationships, or even chase partners who don't respect them, just to avoid feeling alone or unwanted.

3. Loss of Independence: When validation becomes a primary emotional need, people start molding themselves to fit their partner's expectations, sacrificing their own needs, opinions, and desires. They become overly accommodating, fearing that asserting themselves might lead to rejection.
4. Tolerating Mistreatment: People might stay in a relationship where they are belittled or manipulated because leaving would mean losing the one source of validation they've come to rely on.
5. Validation-Seeking Becomes Addictive: When someone receives praise or affection, they feel on top of the world. But when it's withdrawn, they crash, leading to a desperate cycle of trying to "earn" back that validation, often at the cost of their dignity or well-being.

I once knew a man who seemed to have everything going for him—charming, successful, and well-liked. Yet, in every relationship he entered, he constantly sought affirmation. "Do you love me? Do you still find me attractive?" were questions he asked almost daily. At first, his partners saw this as endearing, a sign of his affection. But over time, it became clear that he wasn't asking out of love; he was asking out of fear. His confidence was entirely dependent on external reassurance. The moment his partner stopped reaffirming his worth, he felt unwanted and insecure.

This is the dangerous cycle of validation—it conditions us to seek constant reassurance. At first, it feels good. A partner's praise, affection, and attention can be intoxicating, making us feel special and irreplaceable. But over time, this dependence means that our confidence no longer comes from within. Instead of being grounded in self-awareness and self-acceptance, it becomes tied to how our partner sees us. Every compliment lifts us up, and every moment of indifference or criticism tears us down. Our emotional state becomes a reflection of how much validation we receive.

But what happens when that validation is withdrawn? When the compliments become less frequent? When the attention shifts? When a partner is preoccupied or tired? The illusion of security in the relationship begins to unravel. Suddenly, doubt creeps in. "Are they losing interest?" "Did I do something wrong?" "Am I not good enough?" What once felt like love now feels like uncertainty. The same person who made us feel wanted now has the power to make us feel inadequate.

And this is where the real danger lies—when self-worth is built on validation, any shift in a partner's behavior can feel like rejection. It leads to neediness, overthinking, and even self-sabotage. Some people try harder—seeking ways to regain their partner's attention, bending over backward to be "worthy" again. Others react with resentment, punishing their partner for not providing the validation they crave. Either way, the relationship becomes strained, driven by insecurity rather than genuine connection.

When we rely on a partner to make us feel whole, we give them the power to make us feel broken. The only real solution is to cultivate self-worth from within—to recognize that love should complement us, not complete us.

When validation becomes the driving force in a relationship, the power dynamic shifts. The partner who craves affirmation becomes vulnerable to manipulation. This creates a cycle:

- Partner A constantly seeks validation.

- Partner B provides it but begins to feel burdened.

- Partner B starts withdrawing, feeling suffocated.

- Partner A panics, demands more validation, and the cycle continues.

This whole sequence stirs up a question in me, Does love really need to be proven constantly?

These are my suggestions on how to break free from the validation trap:

- Develop Self-Worth Outside of Relationships: Engage in hobbies, friendships, and personal goals that reinforce your confidence without relying on external approval.
- Recognize When Validation Becomes a Burden: If you find yourself feeling anxious or insecure without constant reassurance, take a step back and ask why.

- Cultivate Emotional Independence: A healthy relationship involves two whole individuals coming together, not two halves seeking completion in each other.
- Communicate Without Clinging: Expressing love should come naturally, not from a place of desperation. A relationship should feel secure even in silence.

Validation in love is not inherently bad; it becomes problematic when it turns into an emotional dependency. True security in relationships comes from mutual respect, emotional stability, and the ability to stand confidently in one's self-worth. Love that is built on needing constant validation is fragile; love that stands on trust and self-assurance is enduring. The strongest relationships are not based on external affirmations but on an internal sense of value—one that exists regardless of whether or not someone is watching.

CHAPTER SIX

THE ILLUSION OF SECURITY

One of the biggest lies we tell ourselves in relationships is that security comes from external guarantees—marriage, financial stability, shared responsibilities, or even just the passage of time. We convince ourselves that if we build a life together, the relationship will last. That if our partner says, "I'll never leave you," or if they post us online, buy us a ring, or promise us forever, we're safe. But security in love has never been about external factors.

True security doesn't come from a wedding band, a joint bank account, or even years spent together. It comes from something far deeper—emotional trust, consistency, and a genuine connection. And when those things are missing, no amount of external stability can make up for it.

I once stayed in a relationship far longer than I should have because I mistook familiarity for security. We had a routine—it felt comfortable. But beneath the surface, I was anxious. I felt like I had to constantly prove myself to maintain the relationship. If I didn't perform, if I didn't meet unspoken expectations, I felt like the love could be taken away.

That's when I realized: The "security" I thought I had was nothing more than an illusion. A structure that looked stable from the outside but was cracking underneath.

We live in a world that sells us a particular story about love. Movies, social media, and even our upbringing teach us that certain milestones equal security. We believe that marriage guarantees a lifelong bond, years together mean emotional closeness, a shared home creates unshakable commitment and/or a partner's words or promises ensure stability.

But do these things really provide security?

I've seen countless relationships where two people had everything society equates with stability—but behind closed doors, they were completely disconnected.

One of my friends used to tell me that every time she said, "What a nice day it is," and her husband ignored her, she'd feel a small stab of anxiety. Her mind would whisper, "If he doesn't care about this, maybe he doesn't care about me."

It might sound small, but small things accumulate. And when major issues—like financial stress, emotional neglect, or lack of intimacy—enter the picture, that illusion of security starts to crumble and the sad truth is that we don't talk enough about how easy it is to feel alone in a relationship. You can be married and still feel unloved.

You can share a home and still feel like strangers. You can have years of history and still feel completely disposable.

Because none of these things actually create security. They only give the illusion of it.

We often assume that hitting certain milestones means our relationship is unbreakable. But here's the hard truth: Security isn't about circumstances. It's about consistency.

Let's break down some of the biggest misconceptions:

1. Marriage = Security

People often assume that once they get married, their relationship will become "real" and secure. But the truth is, marriage doesn't prevent breakups. Some people use marriage as a band-aid for underlying problems I'm thereby proving that a ring doesn't guarantee commitment. Society has painted marriage as the ultimate security blanket. We see it in movies—the grand proposal, the wedding, the promise of happily ever after. But real relationships don't work like fairy tales.

I've seen couples get married hoping it would "fix" their problems—thinking that a commitment on paper would make them feel safe. But security isn't built in a ceremony. It's built in the daily actions, communication, and trust that hold two people together.

2. Time Together = Stability

The longer we're with someone, the more secure we should feel, right? Not necessarily. I know people who have been in relationships for 10+ years and still walk on eggshells. They stay because of history, not because of happiness. Time doesn't guarantee security. If anything, it can create comfort-driven stagnation—where two people stay together not because they truly connect, but because they're afraid to start over.

Security isn't about how long you've been together. It's about how safe you feel within that time.

3. Financial Stability = Emotional Stability

Some people stay in relationships because of financial security. They convince themselves that as long as they share bills, a house, or financial responsibilities, they're secure. But financial stability is not the same as emotional stability. You can rely on someone financially but not trust them emotionally. You can be comfortable, yet deeply unhappy. If financial security is the only thing keeping you in a relationship, that's not security—it's dependence.

4. Public Declarations = Commitment

Social media has made it easy to believe that public affection equals private security. But a post doesn't mean commitment. An engagement announcement doesn't mean loyalty. I've seen relationships where one partner constantly posts about their love online while secretly cheating or emotionally neglecting their partner. Security isn't found in words—it's found in actions that remain steady even when no one is watching.

If security doesn't come from external factors, then where does it come from?

1. Emotional Consistency

Real security is about knowing that your partner's love won't disappear the moment things get hard. It means that they don't manipulate or withhold affection. They communicate openly, rather than shutting down or walking away. They show up for you, even when it's inconvenient.

Security isn't about never having problems. It's about knowing that when problems arise, you'll face them together.

2. Trust That's Proven Over Time

Trust isn't just given—it's earned through repeated actions. A shared mortgage can't replace trust. A wedding ring can't replace reliability. True security comes from:

- A partner who does what they say they will do.
- A relationship where words and actions align.
- Knowing that you don't have to guess how they feel about you.

3. Safe Vulnerability

One of the greatest signs of true security is feeling safe enough to be vulnerable. It means that you can express your fears without judgment. You're allowed to have emotions without fearing abandonment. A truly secure relationship makes emotional intimacy feel safe, not risky.

If you've been holding onto external signs of security, it's time to ask yourself: Do I feel truly safe in this relationship, or am I just afraid of letting go?

HERE'S HOW TO BREAK FREE FROM THE ILLUSION

1. Stop Using Milestones as Proof of Love; Ask yourself, If we stripped away the titles, the marriage, the financial ties—would I still feel emotionally secure in this relationship?
2. Prioritize Emotional Safety Over External Stability: Stability isn't just about staying together—it's about staying connected.
3. Trust Actions Over Words.
4. Stop Settling for Comfort Alone: Don't stay in a relationship just because it's familiar. Comfort and security are not the same thing.

Security is about knowing your partner is truly there for you—not just in words, but in actions. No contract, no ring, no shared mortgage can replace that.

CHAPTER SEVEN

THE ILLUSION OF CONTROL

Some people believe that by manipulating or monitoring all the decisions, they are "protecting" their partner or ensuring their relationship's success. But true love isn't about possession—it's about partnership. A relationship ruled by control, or the need to, equates to emotional suffocation. We may think that by guiding ours and our partner's actions or responses, we can create a sense of stability and predictability. Love should make you (and your partner) feel safe, supported, and free—not trapped. Ask yourself this, *Do I really need autonomous control over everything?*

Let me introduce you to a concept. It describes the tendency to overestimate one's ability to influence or "shape" a partner into an *ideal version of themselves,* focusing more on their potential rather than their actual behavior, leading to unrealistic expectations and eventual disappointment. It reflects a belief that with enough guidance, or effort, one can mold a partner into their desired traits.

Lots of people enter relationships not for what is, but for what could be. They fall in love with potential—the version of their partner they believe will emerge with time, effort, or the right circumstances. A love built on false promises often leads to heartbreak, disappointment, or worse, entrapment in a toxic cycle which is quite dangerous because:

- **You Don't See Red Flags** – When you focus on what could be, you overlook what is. You would begin to make excuses for bad behavior because of some "future" prospective.
- **You Become Their Caretaker In Place Of A Partner** – Love shouldn't feel like a full-time job where you're constantly fixing, or coaching someone or doing all within your power to please and appease your partner to maintain peace.
- **They Have No Reason to Change** – If they're comfortable with the benefits of the relationship (financial, emotional, etc.), they would see no wrong/have no reason for a change.
- **Time is Non-Refundable** – The longer you wait for a change that is quite farfetched, the more invested you become. Which in turn will make it harder to leave—even when it's not working.

Realizing that you've been deceived after a long time can be a deeply painful experience, especially when love had blinded you to the obvious signs. It's even more heartbreaking when a partner—whether male or female—has devoted a significant part of their life to being faithful and loyal, only to realize that their trust was misplaced.

Olivia's experience best fits this description. Olivia, a nurturing and free-spirited, career-oriented and friendly woman, met Mark, a confident, charismatic yet struggling young man that had *potential.* He spoke passionately about his dreams, always had a plan, knew what he wanted and she was totally head over heels for him.

Time passed and Mark's decisiveness casually turned into dominance. He began dictating what Olivia should wear, subtly criticizing her career choices, and insisting that certain friends were "bad influences." At first, his control felt like concern—he just wanted what was best for her, right? Olivia, on the other hand, became one of his biggest supporters, investing all of her in his aspirations because, "he's generally a nice person and his lack of effort isn't because he *wouldn't* improve but because he *couldn't*, yet".

Months turned to years and Mark never built his business or got a stable job. Then came the tracking of apps on her phone, the unspoken rule that she had to answer his calls immediately, the guilt-tripping when she wanted time alone. Whenever she pushed back, Mark reminded her how much he loved her, how the world was dangerous and they needed each other to survive.

One of the most exhausting things in relationships is believing that you can fix someone or that you can control the outcome just by adjusting your behavior. I've seen people—including myself—bend over backward trying to mold themselves into the perfect partner, believing that if they just say the right words, prove their love, or make the right sacrifices, they'll finally get the love they deserve.

But that's not how it works.

A friend of mine was in a toxic relationship for years. His girlfriend constantly manipulated him, making him feel like he was never enough. He thought if he just tried harder, she would finally be satisfied. He lost himself in the process—ignoring his own needs, suppressing his feelings just to keep the peace. But no matter how much he gave, it was never enough.

Like me, my friend had to learn the hard way: You can't control how someone treats you. You can't force them to value you. You can't love them into being better.

I had to learn that real love isn't about controlling the narrative or bending someone's will to fit my desires. Real love flows naturally. It doesn't require chasing, convincing, or constant proving. When I finally let go of the illusion of control, I realized that the right person wouldn't need to be managed—they would choose me just as I was.

CONTROL IS NOT LOVE

- **It Strips Away Individuality** – A relationship should enhance who you are, not erase you. When one person dictates everything, the other loses their sense of self which suppresses/diminishes their uniqueness and identity.
- **Control is Rooted in Insecurity, Not Love** – Mark's behavior wasn't about love—it was about his fear of losing Olivia, so he controlled her instead of trusting her.

- **Love Shouldn't Require Permission** – You should never feel like you need approval to make basic choices about your life, career, or friendships.
- **Isolation is a Warning Sign** – When a partner discourages outside connections, it's a red flag. Healthy love encourages a full, balanced life, not dependence.

CHAPTER EIGHT

THE ILLUSION OF TRUTH

Some people lie to avoid conflict, while others lie simply because they can. Some lies may be harmless or even helpful. Telling your partner that you like their new shirt when you don't care for it, for example, can make your partner feel good, avoid an argument and result in minimal negative repercussions. One thing is for sure, a relationship founded and preserved in lies is like standing on a foundation of sand—sooner or later, everything collapses.

I used to believe that words were enough. If I told someone I loved them, they should believe it. If I swore I'd never lie, they should take my word as fact and vice versa. It took me years—and a lot of pain—to understand that words without actions means nothing.

One of the hardest lessons I learned in relationships was that people can say anything, but it's their behavior that reveals the truth. I once dated someone who was a master at telling me exactly what I wanted to hear. She'd promised commitment, loyalty, and a future together, and she had this way of saying it that made me feel safe. But every time I needed real proof—real effort—there was nothing.

At first, I ignored the signs. I convinced myself that her excuses were valid, that I was overthinking. But deep down, I knew something wasn't right. She would disappear for days, then come back with the sweetest apologies. She'd make plans with me and break them at the last minute. She'd tell me I was the most important person in her life, yet her actions said otherwise.

I see now that I wasn't in love with her—I was in love with the version of her that she created with her words. The illusion of truth.

Some important things to keep in mind is, no matter how carefully constructed, lies don't last forever even small lies create doubt. Liars often make their partners feel crazy for noticing inconsistencies, further damaging emotional security and causing the relationship to suffer.

I've also seen this happen to others. A friend of mine, Emily, fell for someone who convinced her he was emotionally available. He talked about commitment, about building a life together. But when it came to showing up—when she needed him to be present—he always had an excuse. She spent years believing in the potential of their relationship rather than the reality of it.

This pattern is common. We want to believe the best in people, and sometimes that means we ignore what's right in front of us. We hold onto words, hoping that someday they'll match the actions. But hope isn't enough. Love isn't just about promises; it's about follow-through.

IMPORTANT POINTS TO NOTE

1. Words mean nothing without consistent action.
2. When someone repeatedly lets you down, that's not a mistake; it's a pattern.
3. Loving what someone could be is dangerous.
4. Ignoring red flags only prolongs inevitable heartbreak.
5. Truth is in the effort.

Breaking free from the illusion of truth wasn't easy. It required me to let go of wishful thinking and start seeing people for who they truly were. And in doing so, I learned that real love doesn't need illusions—it stands on its own, clear and undeniable.

Truth, in relationships, is often twisted, withheld, or manipulated, not always out of malice, but sometimes out of fear, self-deception, or even love.

I once dated someone who was an expert at telling me just enough of the truth to keep me from questioning her. She never directly lied, but she knew how to spin her words so I would hear what I wanted to believe, rather than what was actually real. I ignored the inconsistencies because I wanted to believe her. I wanted the truth to align with the version of our relationship I had in my head.

The worst lies aren't the ones we tell others. They're the ones we tell ourselves.

Not all dishonesty is outright lying. Some of the most damaging deceptions come in the form of half-truths—when someone tells you just enough to make you feel like they're being honest while leaving out the parts that could change everything.

The illusion of truth is one of the most dangerous traps in relationships. We think we want honesty, but sometimes, we cling to the lies because they're easier to live with. But the truth—no matter how painful—always has a way of coming out. And when it does, it's better to be prepared to face it than to be blindsided by it.

CHAPTER NINE

THE ILLUSION OF CHANGE AND COMPATIBILITY

Some relationships start off feeling perfect, only to reveal deep cracks over time. The problem? People mistake surface-level chemistry for compatibility. Many people believe that if two people love each other enough, they can overcome anything. But love alone doesn't create compatibility. Shared values, life goals, emotional intelligence, and communication matter just as much—if not more—than intense passion.

For the longest time, I believed that chemistry was all that mattered. If the connection was strong, if we laughed at the same jokes and finished each other's sentences, then surely, we were meant to be. But time and experience taught me that compatibility isn't just about attraction, shared interests, or even love—it's about values, lifestyle, and long-term alignment.

One of the easiest traps people fall into in relationships is believing that love can change someone. It's a comforting thought—but the hard truth is that change only happens when a person truly wants it, not when they are pressured, guilted, or begged into it.

I remember a simple argument with my girlfriend at the time. All she wanted was for me to call her back in a timely manner and spend a little more time with her instead of always prioritizing my friends. Instead, I was a complete jerk. I told her she was doing too much and worried about the wrong things, then hung up on her. What worsened the issue was what I did next—I ignored her calls for three days straight, just to prove that I was in control.

By the fourth day, I decided to call her back… but now she was the one ignoring me. Day one—her phone just rang. Day two—same thing. Day three—I was officially panicking. By day four, I swallowed my pride, left an apologetic voicemail promising it wouldn't happen again, and begged her to call me back. She did. But only to tell me it was over. She explained how much I had hurt her and made it clear she had already moved on—with someone else.

That loss stuck with me. But did I really learn from it? Not immediately because I wasn't ready.

Looking back, I realize that real growth isn't just about promising to do better—it's about understanding what better actually looks like. And sometimes, that takes longer than we expect.

We all love a good redemption story. The idea that someone can realize their mistakes, turn their life around, and become the partner they were always meant to be is a powerful fantasy. But in real life, change is rarely that simple.

One of the biggest illusions in relationships is the belief that we can change people. We think that if we love them enough, support them enough, or guide them in the right direction, they'll become the partner we need them to be. But true change doesn't come from external pressure—it comes from within.

A man who cheats won't suddenly become faithful because you forgive him. A woman who disrespects you won't suddenly start valuing you because you stayed. A partner who refuses to take responsibility for their actions won't magically become accountable just because you keep giving them chances.

People change for themselves, not for others. And even then, real transformation takes time, effort, and deep self-awareness.

Another dangerous illusion is the belief that people will grow in the same direction over time. While personal growth is important, it's not guaranteed that two people will evolve in a way that keeps them compatible.

I once dated someone who seemed like my perfect match at the beginning. We shared the same values, wanted the same things, and envisioned a future together. But over the years, we changed—what once felt like perfect alignment slowly turned into a widening gap.

We tried to force it, convincing ourselves that the love we once had meant we were meant to stay together. But the reality was, we had outgrown each other.

IMPORTANT POINTS TO NOTE

1. Chemistry can be misleading. Intense attraction doesn't mean two people are right for each other. Passion can exist even in relationships that are fundamentally flawed.
2. Temporary change is not real change. If someone only improves after a breakup or when they're afraid of losing you, it's not real growth—it's survival mode.
3. The right person won't require you to force compatibility. When you're truly aligned with someone, the relationship flows naturally. You won't have to constantly fight to make things work.
4. Sometimes, the best way to inspire change is to walk away. When you stop enabling bad behavior and remove yourself from toxic situations, it forces people to face the consequences of their actions.
5. You can't save someone who doesn't want to be saved. No amount of love, patience, or sacrifice will fix someone who isn't willing to do the work themselves.

The illusion of change and compatibility keeps people trapped in relationships that feel right but aren't sustainable, waiting for something that will never come. I can understand why people would cling to false change since *the current relationship sector celebrates hope and fear as major ingredients for a successful career*. People would rather hold on to glimpses of a good version than admit they've invested wrongly and it was all for nothing. But when we finally let go of the fantasy and accept people as they are—not as we wish them to be—we free ourselves to find real love, real respect, and real happiness. We open ourselves up to relationships that truly fit—not just in the moment, but for the long haul.

Compromise is necessary, but not at the cost of your happiness.

CHAPTER TEN

THE ILLUSION OF LOYALTY AND SACRIFICE

Loyalty is one of the most cherished values in a relationship. We want to believe that love and commitment go hand in hand and that betrayal is something that only happens to other people. But what if it's not built on genuine devotion, but on fear, obligation, or even manipulation?

I once believed that loyalty meant unwavering commitment, even at the cost of personal happiness. I had a friend, who was in a long-term relationship with a woman who constantly belittled him. She questioned his decisions, made him feel small in front of others, and often threatened to leave when things didn't go her way. Yet, he never walked away.

But the truth was, he was afraid of starting over, of admitting that he had wasted years on someone who didn't truly value him. He wasn't staying because he loved her; he was staying because he was scared to leave.

True loyalty should be rooted in mutual respect and care, not in obligation. There's a fine line between being a committed partner and betraying yourself in the name of staying faithful.

I was once in a relationship where I stayed even after discovering multiple lies. Each time, I told myself, "She didn't mean it," or "She'll change." But the truth is, she never did. I wasn't being loyal—I was ignoring reality.

One of the biggest illusions of loyalty is the idea that sticking it out, no matter what, makes you a better partner. But loyalty should be reciprocated. If you're the only one being faithful, supportive, and committed, then what you have isn't a relationship—it's a one-sided sacrifice.

Sacrifice is often romanticized as the ultimate proof of love. We're told that true love requires giving up parts of ourselves for the sake of our partner. We hear stories of people who endure hardships in relationships, believing that love is about selflessness, about putting someone else's needs before our own. But what happens when sacrifice crosses the line from being an act of love to becoming a slow erasure of self?

I once believed that the more I gave, the stronger the relationship would be. That if I just compromised enough, if I proved my devotion by making sacrifices, things would work out. But over time, I realized something: not all sacrifices are noble. Some are just illusions we create to justify staying in relationships that are draining us.

A friend of mine, Henry, was in a relationship where he constantly gave up his personal happiness for his partner's sake. She didn't like his friends, so he stopped seeing them. She didn't support his career path, so he abandoned it. He told himself that making these sacrifices was what love required and in the long run, he found himself feeling empty. He had given up so much of himself that he no longer recognized who he was. The relationship didn't strengthen—it suffocated.

Sacrificing for a relationship should never mean losing yourself in the process. Love should encourage growth, not demand self-destruction.

Many people fall into the trap of thinking that love should come with endless conditions. "If you love me, you will quit your job and move for me." "If you love me, you will stop talking to certain friends" but real love doesn't require you to prove your devotion by giving up things that are essential to your happiness. Sacrificing should be mutual, not one-sided. If you're the only one giving, while the other takes, then what you have isn't love—it's control masked as devotion.

Signs You're Trapped in the Illusion of Loyalty and Sacrifice

- You feel like you're always the one making adjustments while your partner rarely compromises.
- You've abandoned personal goals or dreams to maintain the relationship.
- You justify your unhappiness by telling yourself that love is about enduring hardship.

- You feel drained, not fulfilled, by your sacrifices.

Redefining Loyalty and Sacrifice in Relationships

Real loyalty is about choosing each other every day because the relationship brings mutual happiness, growth, and respect. Sacrifice should be about balance, not burden. A healthy relationship should be built on mutual understanding, where both partners are willing to adjust for the sake of harmony—but never at the cost of their own identity. If staying in a relationship means sacrificing your peace, your values, or your self-worth, then it's not loyalty—it's self-betrayal. Loyalty should never mean losing yourself.

Love should never demand that you give up who you are. If it does, then it's an illusion.

CHAPTER ELEVEN

THE ILLUSION OF COMMITMENT AND STABILITY

Commitment and stability—two words that often define the foundation of a lasting relationship. We seek them, cling to them, and measure our relationships by their presence. Society teaches us that these are the hallmarks of a successful partnership: the idea that once someone commits to you, whether through marriage, cohabitation, or even verbal promises, stability will follow. But the truth is, commitment and stability, in their traditional sense, can be illusions.

I've seen relationships that looked perfect from the outside, but behind closed doors, they were fragile, held together by routine rather than genuine emotional connection. I've been in situations where I mistook consistency for stability, believing that as long as things didn't change dramatically, the relationship was solid. But the reality is that true commitment is not about the mere act of staying—it's about choosing each other every day, even when it's difficult. And stability is not about avoiding change but about growing together through it.

Many people believe that once they define a relationship—whether through exclusivity, engagement, or marriage—commitment is guaranteed. The title of 'boyfriend,' 'girlfriend,' 'husband,' or 'wife' creates an illusion of permanence. But a label does not ensure loyalty, nor does it prevent emotional or physical betrayal.

I once knew a couple that had been married for years. To everyone, they seemed happy, their life together a picture of stability but behind that illusion, they lived as strangers. They no longer shared their thoughts, desires, or fears. The husband traveled often for work, and the wife found solace in her social circles. They stayed together not because they were committed to each other but because they feared the chaos of separation. Their commitment was to keep up appearances, not to their emotional well-being.

This isn't an uncommon scenario. Many relationships persist because of fear—fear of loneliness, of financial strain, or of judgment from others. But staying together for these reasons isn't stability; it's entrapment.

People often mistake a lack of conflict for stability. They believe that if they aren't fighting, if they follow the same routines, if things feel comfortable, then their relationship is stable. But stability isn't about avoiding disruption—it's about the ability to navigate it together. There was a time when I stayed in a relationship simply because it was steady. We rarely argued, we shared expenses, and our lives had intertwined in a way that felt permanent. But beneath that surface, something was missing. The emotional connection had faded, replaced by a silent agreement to coexist. We weren't growing, we weren't deepening our bond—we were just there.

True stability should come from a shared commitment to each other's growth, even when it's uncomfortable. It means having difficult conversations, challenging each other's perspectives, and facing changes head-on rather than pretending they don't exist.

Think of it like a job. Some people show up every day, clocking in and out, but they aren't engaged. They don't contribute ideas, they don't strive for growth—they simply exist within the system. Relationships can function the same way. A partner can stay physically present while being emotionally absent. That being said, commitment should not be measured by how long someone stays, but by how much they invest in making the relationship thrive. Do they communicate openly? Do they support your dreams and personal growth? Do they make an effort to keep the connection alive?

If the answer to these questions is no, then their presence is merely an illusion of commitment.

I knew a man who stayed in a relationship for five years longer than he wanted to because he and his partner had a house together. Leaving meant dealing with lawyers, financial losses, and the shame of admitting their relationship had failed. They slept in separate rooms, led separate lives, but remained a couple in the eyes of the world.

These external factors create an illusion of stability. But real stability isn't about shared assets—it's about emotional security. When two people can trust each other fully, communicate openly, and support each other's growth, that's real stability. No house, no joint bank account, no social status can replace that.

You see, when we buy into the illusion of commitment and stability, we often delay necessary decisions but in doing so, we rob ourselves of the opportunity for true happiness.

A woman I once worked with stayed in a toxic relationship because she had invested so many years into it. She believed that if she just held on a little longer, things would get better. But time alone doesn't fix a relationship—effort does. And when effort is one-sided, no amount of waiting will create the stability she longed for.

The first step to breaking free from the illusion of commitment and stability is self-awareness. Ask yourself:

Am I in this relationship because I truly want to be, or because I fear leaving?

Does my partner actively invest in our relationship, or are they just present?

Once you acknowledge the truth, you can take action. It doesn't always mean leaving a relationship—it could mean having deeper conversations, setting new expectations, or working together to rebuild what's been lost. But if the relationship is held together only by obligation, fear, or convenience, then it may be time to walk away.

Remember that commitment and stability, when real, are beautiful things. But when they exist only in appearance, they become traps. Love should not feel like an obligation. Stability should not feel like stagnation. And commitment should not feel like a cage. If we let go of the illusion, we open ourselves up to the possibility of something real—something built not on fear, but on love, trust, and genuine connection.

CHAPTER TWELVE

THE ILLUSION OF EMOTIONAL INTELLIGENCE

Emotional intelligence is often praised as the cornerstone of a successful relationship. We admire partners who seem self-aware, who express themselves eloquently, and who appear to understand our feelings. But sometimes, what we perceive as emotional intelligence could be a facade, a well-rehearsed performance, a carefully crafted illusion that makes us believe someone is more emotionally mature than they truly are. I can say this confidently because I have confirmed it.

I once dated someone who spoke fluently about emotions. She could analyze every situation, breaking down our conflicts with remarkable precision. It was impressive—until I realized that understanding emotions and truly feeling them are two very different things. She knew how to say the right things, but when it came to genuine empathy and action, she fell short. She was great at apologizing but never actually changed her behavior.

This is where many people get trapped in the illusion. Just because someone can talk about their feelings—or yours—doesn't mean they are emotionally responsible. Real emotional intelligence isn't just about acknowledging emotions; it's about acting in a way that nurtures the relationship. This illusion often presents itself in subtle ways. Here are some red flags:

1. Overanalyzing Without Action – They can dissect a problem and explain why it happened, but they do nothing to fix it.
2. Apologizing Without Change – They apologize frequently but continue the same harmful behaviors.
3. Using Psychology to Deflect Responsibility – They rationalize their toxic behavior by diagnosing themselves or you, making it seem like they're self-aware when they're just avoiding accountability.
4. Manipulating Through "Understanding" – They use their emotional awareness as a weapon, making you feel like you're the problem while appearing calm and rational.
5. Lack of Consistency – They can be emotionally available when it suits them but distant when you need them most.

You could be thinking, these are quite common red flags, why then do we fall for it? My answer is also cliché.

We all want a partner who "gets" us. When someone seems emotionally intelligent, we assume they are also kind, mature, and capable of deep love. But intelligence, whether intellectual or emotional, doesn't always translate to emotional wisdom. Someone can be articulate about emotions yet completely lack the ability to build a healthy relationship.

I've seen friends stay in relationships because their partner "talks about their emotions" or "seems so introspective." But introspection without emotional accountability is just self-indulgence. Love isn't about who can win the argument with logic.

Being with someone who appears emotionally intelligent but lacks true emotional depth can leave you feeling drained. You may question your own emotions because your partner seems to have a logical explanation for everything. You may find yourself trapped in endless discussions that go nowhere, as your partner skillfully avoids making real changes.

This illusion can also make you feel like you're the unreasonable one. If your partner presents themselves as calm, rational, and self-aware while dismissing your feelings, you might start doubting your own reality. This is a form of subtle manipulation, and over time, it can erode your self-esteem. Therefore, real emotional intelligence isn't about appearing calm or knowing all the right psychological terms—it's about demonstrating emotional responsibility in everyday actions. A truly emotionally intelligent partner:

- Listens with the intent to understand, not just to respond.

- Validates emotions without dismissing them or making excuses.

- Is willing to be vulnerable without using it as a manipulation tactic.

- Takes accountability and follows through with genuine change.

- Creates emotional safety rather than using emotions as a tool for control.

If you've found yourself in a relationship where emotional intelligence is just a performance, it's time to reassess. Ask yourself: Are they using their self-awareness to grow, or just to justify their flaws?

In love, words matter—but actions matter more.

CHAPTER THIRTEEN

THE ILLUSION OF EFFORT

As a man, I've learned that effort in relationships is a tricky thing. We grow up hearing that relationships take work, but what does that really mean? Some people believe that as long as they're putting in some effort, the relationship should thrive. They assume that doing the bare minimum—checking in once a day, remembering birthdays, or saying "I love you"—is enough to sustain a deep connection. But effort isn't just about doing things; it's about doing the right things with consistency and intent.

I once thought I was making an effort in a relationship, but in reality, I was just going through the motions. I did things that I thought counted as effort, like buying gifts when I messed up, planning a date night every now and then, or remembering to compliment her when she looked particularly stunning. But I never asked myself the important question—was I making an effort in the way she needed? Was I truly present, engaged, and proactive? Or was I just keeping score?

Many men, myself included at one point, fall into the trap of thinking that as long as we're "doing things," we're making an effort. But there's a difference between going through the motions and truly investing in a relationship. The problem is that many relationships function on autopilot—where one or both partners assume that their mere presence or occasional gestures are enough.

Example of the bare minimum: Replying to messages, planning a date when reminded, apologizing without genuine change, buying gifts to make up for mistakes.

Example of true effort: Being emotionally present, listening actively, remembering details that matter to your partner, putting in work to resolve conflicts instead of sweeping them under the rug.

There are lots of men out there that were never taught how to express deep emotional effort. Society often conditions us to believe that providing financially, fixing things around the house, or offering logical solutions to problems are the primary ways to show care. But real effort means understanding what your partner needs, not just what you think should be enough.

One of the most dangerous illusions is when one partner believes they're putting in effort, but their actions don't translate into actual emotional connection. This often happens in relationships where one person is emotionally unavailable but still "does things" to maintain the relationship.

I remember a friend who was stuck in this cycle. He did what he thought were grand gestures—weekend getaways, expensive dinners, occasional compliments—but he was emotionally distant. His partner felt neglected, unheard, and frustrated. To him, he was "trying." To her, he was absent. His effort was performative, not meaningful.

Effort in relationships should be mutual and organic, not a calculated exchange. If a man constantly feels like he's "doing things" just to get something in return—be it affection, sex, or validation—it stops being genuine effort and becomes a transaction. This breeds resentment because real connection isn't about keeping score; it's about wanting to do things for your partner simply because you care.

I once fell into the habit of thinking, I planned a nice date, so why is she still upset? or I told her she looked beautiful, why isn't she happy? It took me a while to realize that true effort isn't about checking off a list; it's about consistently showing up and understanding your partner's needs without expecting immediate rewards.

A lack of emotional intelligence can make effort feel like a mystery to some men. If you don't take the time to understand your partner—her triggers, her love language, her fears—your effort will always be misplaced. No amount of fancy dinners will make up for a lack of emotional depth. I'll give you some ways to show real effort:

1. Listening actively – not just hearing words, but understanding emotions behind them.
2. Following through on promises – reliability is a major part of showing commitment.

3. Noticing small things – remembering her favorite coffee order, the way she wrings her hands when anxious, the shows she loves.
4. Being proactive in emotional labor – addressing issues before they become fights, checking in on her well-being without being prompted.
5. Adjusting, not just apologizing – a true apology means a change in behavior, not just saying sorry to end an argument.

The illusion of effort can keep people trapped in stagnant relationships where one or both partners believe they're "trying," but nothing ever changes. The truth is, effort isn't about quantity; it's about quality. You can't half-love someone and expect the relationship to flourish.

Looking back, I now realize that real effort is about understanding that love isn't about grand declarations but about consistency, presence, and genuine investment in another person's happiness.

No one should settle for an illusion when real love, built on mutual effort, is possible.

CHAPTER FOURTEEN

THE ILLUSION OF MUTUAL GROWTH

Growth is one of the most attractive aspects of a relationship. We enter relationships believing that we will evolve together, that our partner will grow at the same pace we do, and that we will become better versions of ourselves because of each other. This belief is comforting, even inspiring. It gives relationships a sense of purpose beyond love and companionship. But more often than not, the idea of mutual growth is an illusion—one that traps people in stagnant, toxic, or one-sided relationships, hoping for a change that may never come.

Many people believe that love naturally pushes both partners to grow in harmony. The reality, however, is that individual growth is unpredictable. People develop at different speeds, in different directions, and under different circumstances. Just because two people start on the same path doesn't mean they will remain aligned forever.

I once believed that being in a committed relationship meant both of us would grow at the same rate. I expected that as I worked on my emotional intelligence, she would too. As I became more financially disciplined, she would also make strides in her ambitions. But time proved otherwise. While I was striving for self-improvement, she remained comfortable in the status quo. And yet, I kept waiting, convincing myself that any day now, she would change, that we would reach the same level, that she would see what I saw. But that day never came.

The danger of believing in mutual growth is that one partner often ends up carrying the weight of progress. One person may read books on self-development, work on communication skills, or strive to become a better version of themselves, while the other remains complacent, either unaware or unwilling to put in the same effort.

Many relationships suffer because one partner assumes that love alone is enough to motivate the other to change. But love is not a catalyst for personal transformation. No one changes unless they are personally motivated to do so, and waiting for someone to evolve on your timeline is one of the biggest mistakes you can make.

When one person in a relationship continues to grow while the other remains the same, resentment builds. The growing partner starts to feel frustrated, unappreciated, or even burdened by the lack of progress in their partner. This resentment is subtle at first—a lingering disappointment when they realize they can no longer have stimulating conversations, a feeling of isolation when they see others achieving goals together. But over time, it becomes suffocating.

I remember feeling like I was constantly dragging my partner forward, pushing her to aim higher, to do better, to see the bigger picture. But instead of mutual effort, I was met with excuses, resistance, or outright avoidance. The weight of carrying someone else's potential is exhausting. I reached a point where I had to ask myself: Am I in love with the person she is, or the potential I hope she reaches?

One of the harshest lessons in love is that growth should never be conditional. You shouldn't improve yourself just to match your partner's expectations, nor should you expect someone to change simply because you are growing. Personal development is an independent journey. You can encourage, inspire, or support your partner, but you cannot force them to evolve.

Many people stay in unfulfilling relationships because they convince themselves that their partner is "almost there". That with just a little more patience, a little more sacrifice, things will finally fall into place. But the reality is that if someone wanted to grow, they would do so with or without you. Your relationship should enhance your growth, not be a requirement for it.

The hardest decision to make is walking away from someone you love simply because they aren't growing in the same direction as you. But staying in a stagnant relationship out of loyalty to the past is a disservice to both people involved. When I finally accepted that my partner was not invested in growth, I had to make a choice—stay and compromise my own progress, or leave and allow myself to continue evolving. It was one of the most difficult decisions I ever made, but in hindsight, it was necessary. The illusion of mutual growth had kept me in a space where I was emotionally and mentally drained, constantly waiting for something that was never going to happen.

A truly healthy relationship is one where both partners are individually growing while supporting each other's journey. There is no pressure, no waiting in vain. Growth is natural, mutual, and self-motivated. It isn't dictated by love alone but by personal drive, ambition, and a desire for self-improvement. When two people are genuinely growing together, they are aligned in mindset, goals, and emotional intelligence. They hold each other accountable, celebrate each other's wins, and respect the individuality of their growth paths. There is no illusion—only reality, effort, and commitment to bettering themselves for the sake of their own lives, not just for the relationship.

The illusion of mutual growth convinces people to stay in relationships that no longer serve them, hoping for a future that may never materialize. But true security in love comes from knowing that you and your partner are evolving, not because you have to, but because you want to. A relationship should be a space where two whole individuals support each other's progress, not where one person waits endlessly for the other to catch up.

CHAPTER FIFTEEN

THE ILLUSION OF FORGIVENESS

Forgiveness is often seen as the ultimate act of love, the thing that holds relationships together when everything else starts to fall apart. We're told that if we truly love someone, we should be willing to forgive them. But what happens when forgiveness becomes a way to excuse toxic behavior, to keep the relationship intact at all costs, even when it's no longer healthy?

I once dated a woman who was a master at apologies. She knew exactly what to say after she hurt me—how to make her remorse sound deep and sincere, how to promise she would change. And every time, I forgave her, I told myself that love required patience, that nobody was perfect, that I should focus on the good in her rather than the mistakes she made. Until I realized that I wasn't actually forgiving her—I was just resetting the cycle.

True forgiveness is acknowledging the hurt, learning from it, and making sure it doesn't happen again while false forgiveness—on the other hand, is when someone apologizes just enough to move past the issue but not enough to actually grow from it.

People often hold onto the illusion of forgiveness because they fear what's on the other side of it and I find that today's relationships are mostly fueled by fear. Some are:

- Fear of conflict
- Fear of being alone
- Fear of looking "unforgiving"

Not everyone deserves your forgiveness. Some people mistake it for permission to hurt you again.

If someone keeps breaking your trust, forgiveness won't fix the issue—distance will. If they apologize but dismiss your pain, they don't truly regret what they did. If their actions repeatedly make you question your self-worth, it's time to walk away.

True forgiveness is a gift, it should never be used as a tool to keep a broken relationship alive. Real love doesn't demand endless chances—it values and respects the first one. Empathy which helps people understand the pain of others and compassion which motivates people to help relieve that suffering are qualities that can help facilitate the forgiveness process.

STEPS TO SELF-FORGIVENESS:

- Acknowledge feelings: Recognizing my emotions, understanding that they are signals, not weaknesses and giving myself *grace* helped me realize that I needed to accept my feelings in order to understand it.
- Label reasons for guilt: One of the ways I realized what I was feeling truly and deeply was by calling it as it is. Why do I feel the way I feel? Note it down.
- Apologize to oneself and others: "I'm sorry" shouldn't be a tough vocabulary to use.
- Show oneself compassion: feeling sorry for oneself isn't as pathetic as it is sometimes made to seem. Be kind yourself, you're not the first to make mistakes.
- Think about how to grow: how to handle situations differently, navigating emotions better.. etc.
- Remember that change takes time: it won't happen in a beat of a heart. Give yourself time to learn and understand the process.
- Forgive oneself.

Not all forgiveness is created equal. There's a difference between forgiveness that leads to healing and forgiveness that keeps you trapped.

Real Forgiveness	Illusory Forgiveness
The person acknowledges the full impact of their actions.	The same mistakes keep happening.
They take real steps to change, not just say "sorry."	Forgiveness is expected, not earned.
They don't pressure you to "move on" before you're ready.	You feel guilty for still feeling hurt.
You feel peace after forgiving, not resentment.	Their apology is just a tool to reset the relationship, not repair it.

CHAPTER SIXTEEN

THE ILLUSION OF REDEMPTION

One of the most dangerous illusions in relationships is the belief that love can fix everything. That if you just love someone enough, they will change. That past mistakes can be undone through patience, commitment, and sacrifice. That a broken relationship can be repaired simply because both people want it to work. This is the illusion of redemption, and it has kept countless individuals trapped in cycles of dysfunction, toxicity, and heartbreak.

As men, we are often taught to be the fixers, the protectors, the ones who hold everything together. We take on the weight of our partner's struggles, convinced that if we just provide enough stability, if we love hard enough, if we show them what real commitment looks like, they will finally see the light and become the person we need them to be. But reality doesn't work that way. Love is not a magic cure. It cannot erase deep-seated issues, nor can it turn someone into a version of themselves they aren't willing to become.

Let's briefly talk about the *Savior Complex*. Many men fall into the trap of trying to "save" their partner. Perhaps she has trust issues from past relationships, or she is emotionally unavailable, or she struggles with self-worth. Whatever the case, we convince ourselves that we can be different, that we can be the ones to show her that not all men are the same. We pour everything into proving that we are reliable, trustworthy, and willing to do whatever it takes to make the relationship work.

But here's the hard truth: a person who does not want to change will not change, no matter how much love you give them. Change is a personal journey, one that cannot be forced upon someone. You cannot love someone into being whole, you cannot fix them with your devotion. And more often than not, in trying to do so, you end up losing yourself in the process.

The illusion of redemption also manifests in relationships where mistakes have been made—betrayal, dishonesty, emotional neglect. A partner who has cheated promises to never do it again. A partner who has been emotionally distant vows to finally open up. And for a while, things might improve. But if the core issues that led to those behaviors are not addressed, the cycle repeats itself.

It's easy to cling to the good moments, to hold onto the idea that things are getting better, even when the evidence says otherwise. You start excusing behaviors, justifying red flags, and convincing yourself that progress—no matter how small—is a sign that the relationship is worth saving. You believe in their potential more than their reality, and in doing so, you keep yourself stuck in a relationship that will never truly give you what you need.

Holding onto this illusion often means sacrificing your own happiness, your own mental health, and your own needs in the process. You stay in situations that drain you emotionally and physically, thinking that your endurance will eventually lead to a breakthrough. But what if that breakthrough never comes? What if, in trying to save someone else, you lose yourself?

You might find yourself tolerating disrespect, bending your boundaries, and justifying behavior that, deep down, you know isn't right. You tell yourself that love requires patience, that real relationships are hard work, and that walking away means you didn't try hard enough. But in reality, love should never require you to abandon yourself. A healthy relationship is built on mutual effort and growth, not one person constantly trying to redeem the other.

True redemption in a relationship does not come from one partner trying to fix the other. It comes from both individuals recognizing their own flaws, taking accountability, and making a conscious effort to improve—not because they are being pushed, but because they genuinely want to. It comes from open communication, self-awareness, and a willingness to address the root causes of the issues at hand.

If someone is truly willing to change, they will do so whether you are in their life or not. They won't need to be convinced or coerced. They will take the necessary steps on their own because they recognize the importance of growth and healing. And that is the difference between real redemption and the illusion of it.

The hardest part of breaking free from the illusion of redemption is accepting that sometimes, love is not enough. That sometimes, no matter how much history you share, how deep your connection feels, or how much potential you see, the healthiest thing you can do is walk away. Letting go does not mean you failed. It does not mean you didn't love hard enough or try hard enough. It means you respect yourself enough to choose a relationship that does not require you to prove your worth over and over again.

Real love does not need saving. Real love does not require one person to fix another. It is built on mutual trust, effort, and emotional safety and when those elements are missing, no amount of hope, patience, or endurance will ever be enough to create a healthy relationship.

So if you find yourself holding onto someone because you believe in what they could be rather than who they are, ask yourself this: Are you truly in love with them, or are you in love with the idea of what they might become?

CHAPTER SEVENTEEN

THE ILLUSION OF CLOSURE

Closure is a concept often romanticized in relationships, as if it's a neat, final conversation that grants peace and understanding. Many believe that closure is the key to moving on—that once we have all the answers, we can finally let go. But in reality, closure is not something that can always be given by another person. More often than not, the pursuit of closure becomes an endless loop of seeking validation, reliving pain, and waiting for something that may never come.

We've seen it in movies—the dramatic final conversation, where both parties walk away with mutual understanding, a sense of peace, and no lingering questions. In reality, breakups rarely unfold this way. More often, they end in confusion, unanswered questions, and emotional turmoil. Expecting a relationship to end with perfect clarity is an illusion that keeps many people trapped in the past, searching for something that may not exist.

In my experience, I've seen people beg for closure when, in reality, they were seeking an opportunity to rekindle the relationship. They weren't looking for understanding—they were looking for hope.

But the truth is, if someone wanted to stay, they would. If they chose to leave, the answers they provide won't change that decision.

One of the biggest traps of the closure illusion is the belief that if we just understood why someone left or why things didn't work out, we could move on but relationships are rarely that simple. People leave for reasons they themselves don't always fully understand. Sometimes, they may not even be honest about their reasons, either because they don't want to hurt you or because they are avoiding their own guilt. Think about it—how many times have you replayed a breakup in your head, analyzing every detail, every conversation, every moment? Did it bring peace, or did it pull you deeper into the emotional storm? Understanding the why doesn't erase the pain. It often prolongs it.

There's also an unspoken power dynamic in the concept of closure. The person who seeks it is often the one who was left behind, while the one who left holds all the answers. This imbalance makes closure feel like a reward you must earn from the person who hurt you. But true closure is not something they can give—it is something you must claim for yourself. Waiting for someone to explain their actions, apologize, or offer comfort after they've hurt you is like handing them the power to decide when you get to heal. And the longer you wait, the more you prolong your own suffering. The conversation doesn't bring peace; it brings old emotions rushing back. The person may not say what you wanted to hear. They may be indifferent, or worse, they may manipulate your emotions all over again.

I've seen people go back to toxic relationships because they thought they needed closure, only to be trapped in a cycle of leaving and returning. The moment they think they've moved on, the other person reappears, dangling false hope in front of them. This cycle isn't closure—it's emotional entrapment.

The truth is, real closure comes from within. It is a decision, not a conversation. It's the moment you stop seeking answers from someone else and start creating your own. You need to:

- Accept that you may never get all the answers. Not every ending needs a clear explanation. Some things just are.
- Focus on self-healing, not external validation. Journaling, therapy, and self-reflection are more effective in healing than waiting for someone else to give you peace.
- Cut ties completely. Social media stalking, checking their updates, or keeping the door open for communication only delays healing.
- Understand that closure is not a feeling; it's a decision. The moment you decide to move on, you create your own closure.

The idea that closure comes from someone else is an illusion that keeps people emotionally tethered to their past. True closure is the realization that you don't need another person to validate your pain or give you permission to move forward. You choose to heal, to accept, and to let go—not because someone explained their actions, but because you deserve peace. Closure isn't a door someone else closes for you. It's the moment you decide to walk away, lock it yourself, and throw away the key.

CHAPTER EIGHTEEN

THE ILLUSION OF READINESS

Many people enter relationships believing they are ready simply because they desire companionship, love, or validation. However, readiness is not defined by how much you crave intimacy or how lonely you feel. True readiness comes from a place of emotional maturity, self-awareness, and the ability to maintain a relationship beyond the honeymoon phase.

The illusion of readiness often leads people into toxic cycles where they enter relationships unprepared, only to realize later that they lack the emotional or mental tools to sustain them. They confuse infatuation for preparedness, believing that finding the "right" person will automatically lead to a successful relationship. But in reality, relationships demand a level of preparedness that goes beyond fleeting emotions or romantic ideals. Before engaging in an exclusive relationship, both men and women should follow fundamental guidelines to ensure they are entering from a place of strength, not desperation. Below are key pillars of relationship readiness:

- Wisdom with Silence: Before you can truly understand another person, you must first understand yourself. Silence allows introspection—self-reflection on past experiences, mistakes, and lessons but many people fear silence and rush into relationships to avoid loneliness. However, taking time to be alone and learn from past failures is crucial. Wisdom comes from studying relationships (both personal and observed) and learning from them.

- Listening: A strong relationship requires the ability to actively listen rather than just hear. Many people listen to respond instead of listening to understand. It is common knowledge that poor listening leads to miscommunication, assumptions, and eventual breakdowns in relationships but sharp listening skills allow you to detect inconsistencies, understand your partner's emotions, and navigate conflicts effectively.
- Thoughtfulness: Being ready for a relationship means understanding that communication is not just about expressing your needs but also about remembering and respecting your partner's. Small details matter—remembering birthdays, preferences, dislikes, and past conversations builds emotional intimacy. Without intentional communication, relationships become shallow and transactional.

Many people commit before they are truly ready, mistaking desire for preparedness. This leads to the following consequences:

- Mistaking Infatuation for Readiness: Being physically attracted or emotionally invested does not mean you are ready for the responsibility that comes with commitment. Infatuation is intense but temporary—it does not guarantee long-term compatibility.

- The Role of Past Trauma and Unhealed Wounds: Many people enter relationships with unresolved emotional baggage, expecting their partner to "fix" them. Unhealed wounds undoubtedly leads to projecting fears and insecurities onto a partner, creating unnecessary conflicts.
- Seeking Validation Instead of Partnership: Some people enter relationships not because they want a healthy bond, but because they need external validation. I must repeat that a relationship should not be a source of self-worth—it should complement your existing confidence.

Before committing to an exclusive relationship, ask yourself: Have I defined my boundaries? Am I willing to make compromises without losing myself? Do I understand the weight of commitment?

THE ILLUSION VS THE REALITY OF READINESS

The Illusion	**The Reality:**
"I want love, so I must be ready for it".	Readiness isn't about wanting love—it's about being emotionally stable enough to handle its ups and downs.

“I’ll change once I meet the right person”.	A relationship cannot fix you; you must enter it as a whole person.
“Love should complete me”.	Compatibility and effort matter more than the idea of finding “the one.”
“We’ll figure things out as we go”.	Preparation involves learning, healing, and growing before stepping into a relationship.

The illusion of readiness often leads people into heartbreak because they mistake desire for preparation. True readiness is not about wanting love—it’s about being capable of maintaining it. By seeking wisdom, refining communication, and practicing self-awareness, you increase your chances of building a relationship that is fulfilling, balanced, and built on a strong foundation.

CHAPTER NINETEEN

THE ILLUSION OF BALANCE

Balance is often portrayed as one of the cornerstones of a successful relationship. The idea is simple: when two people are perfectly aligned—emotionally, mentally, and physically—they form a harmonious partnership. This illusion of balance suggests that once you meet the "right" person, everything will simply fall into place, with each partner complementing the other perfectly.

However, relationships are rarely as smooth as we envision. While balance is indeed a key element, the illusion of it leads many to believe that true love is about constant equilibrium, where every need is met perfectly without conflict. In reality, achieving balance in a relationship takes conscious effort, compromise, and an understanding that it's not about perfection—it's about navigating the inherent complexities together.

In the beginning, we often believe that love means being equal in every aspect—whether it's emotional contribution, responsibilities, or effort. The illusion is that both partners should give exactly the same amount, creating a *perfectly mirrored partnership.* This leads to unrealistic expectations of fairness and equity that can be damaging to the relationship. Expecting everything to be equally divided is unrealistic. For example, one person may handle the emotional labor while the other takes on financial responsibilities. The key is the willingness to adjust and compensate when needed. In fact, at different times, one partner may give more in certain areas while the other compensates in others.

Fairness in relationships is not about equal exchanges but about balance. Sometimes, one partner may go through a challenging period (emotionally or physically), and the other needs to step up and carry the load temporarily. There will be times when one person needs more, and that doesn't mean the balance is off. Understanding that it's okay for one partner to need extra support without creating a scorecard of contributions is essential.

The expectation of fairness can lead to an unhealthy "tit-for-tat" mentality, leading to competition rather than cooperation.

One of the most shared myths in relationships is that both partners should have equal control or influence over decisions, behaviors, and outcomes. In truth, relationships are inherently dynamic, and power shifts occur depending on various factors such as emotional states, external stressors, or life events.

Power balance does not mean both people always hold the same amount of influence. At times, one partner may take the lead—whether in decision-making, planning, or offering emotional guidance. The relationship thrives when both partners are flexible and willing to give each other space to lead at different times. It's important to understand that true balance doesn't demand rigid equality in power but a sense of fairness and respect in how decisions are made and responsibilities are shared.

Trusting your partner with autonomy and individuality allows both people to grow independently while maintaining a strong connection. Insecure control leads to resentment and stunted growth.

Another common misconception is that a balanced relationship means both partners should always be happy but in reality, relationships require ongoing effort, but not every moment is going to be filled with joy or contentment.

Relationships require constant work, but that doesn't mean it should feel like a struggle all the time. True balance comes when both partners are committed to maintaining the relationship through good times and bad. This doesn't mean "fixing" each other or always agreeing—it means making an effort to understand each other's needs and work together toward mutual goals.

The illusion of effortless love leads to dissatisfaction when problems arise. Every relationship faces challenges, and it's through working together that true balance is achieved.

Happiness in relationships is not a constant state—it flows. Expecting constant joy and fulfillment from your partner is unrealistic and can place undue pressure on the relationship. A balanced relationship involves acknowledging that there will be tough moments and difficult emotions. What matters is how both partners navigate these lows—whether they support each other, communicate, and continue to nurture the relationship.

Many people mistake long-term stability for perfect balance. They believe that once they've established a relationship, it should be smooth sailing from there on out. This misconception creates unrealistic expectations and often leads to disappointment when inevitable challenges arise. Relationships should be a safe space for growth, both individually and as a couple.

Resilience in a relationship means being able to weather the storms together—learning to negotiate, compromise, and even let go of expectations that cause unnecessary friction.

Achieving true balance doesn't mean creating a perfectly harmonious partnership at all times—it means being able to navigate the inevitable flows, supporting each other through challenges, and allowing space for individual growth. True balance is a journey, not a destination. By rejecting the myth of perfection and embracing the fluidity of love, we can create lasting, meaningful relationships built on a foundation of understanding and mutual support.

RECIPE FOR A BRILLIANT RELATIONSHIP

As a man, I've learned that a brilliant relationship doesn't just happen. It's something that takes effort, wisdom, patience, and above all, intention. Too often, we think that love is supposed to be easy or automatic. We see the movies, hear the stories, and believe that the right person will somehow make everything fall into place. But the truth is, a successful relationship is built on a foundation of conscious choices and actions. I've put together a recipe for what I believe makes a brilliant relationship—one that's built on mutual respect, emotional intelligence, and shared goals. These are the principles I've found to be most effective in creating a partnership that not only survives but thrives.

1. Seek Wisdom through Silence

Before you can truly build a healthy, strong relationship, you need to understand yourself first. This is a principle I've come to embrace: seek wisdom by first seeking silence. In our fast-paced world, where we're constantly bombarded with noise—social media, work pressures, family dynamics—it's easy to forget the importance of slowing down and reflecting. Silence isn't just the absence of sound, it's the absence of distractions, the moment where you can tune into yourself.

I've learned that the best way to prepare for a relationship is to understand my own values, needs, and goals. Silence gives me the space to recognize my strengths and weaknesses, the areas where I still need to grow, and what I'm truly seeking in a partner.

This is where emotional maturity begins. You can't give your best self to someone else if you don't understand yourself in the first place. This doesn't mean being alone forever, but carving out moments to listen to your inner voice and truly reflect on what you want out of life and love.

2. Sharpen Your Listening Skills

Listening is one of the most important, yet underrated, skills you can bring into any relationship. I've learned the hard way that it's not enough just to hear what my partner is saying. I need to truly listen. Active listening goes beyond just hearing words—it's about understanding emotions, reading body language, and picking up on what's not being said. It's a sign of respect. When my partner speaks, I make an intentional effort to truly absorb what she's feeling and communicating, without interruption or distraction.

This goes hand in hand with empathy. You can't be emotionally available for your partner if you're not attuned to their needs, concerns, and feelings. It's about creating a space where both partners feel heard and understood. When listening becomes a practice, you move from a place of simple conversation to true emotional connection.

3. Practice Communication

The next key ingredient in a brilliant relationship is communication—and more importantly, remembrance. Communication isn't just about talking; it's about sharing honestly and openly. I've found that healthy communication allows us to express our feelings, needs, and desires without fear of judgment or rejection. But even more than that, communication in a brilliant relationship is about listening and remembering the small things—like how your partner likes their coffee or the things that make them smile—builds intimacy. It's the small gestures of thoughtfulness that make a difference.

And I don't just mean remembering your partner's likes or dislikes—I'm talking about remembering the moments that matter, the things that have been shared in conversations, the promises you've made. When I show my partner that I remember what's important to her, I show her that I value her and our connection.

4. Practice What You Preach

One of the hardest lessons I've learned is that actions speak louder than words. It's easy to tell your partner what you want them to do, but it's far more impactful when you show up by doing those same things yourself.

I used to think that simply voicing my expectations was enough. But if I want respect, I need to show respect. If I expect honesty, I need to be open and truthful myself. A brilliant relationship is built on mutual accountability. I've learned that in order to ask for the best from my partner, I need to give my best, consistently.

A lot of men struggle with this, but it's about leading by example. If I want to be loved and understood, I need to show that same level of love and understanding. Relationships are a mirror, and they reflect what we put into them.

5. Be the Teacher and the Student

A successful relationship isn't just about two people existing together—it's about growing together. Being a teacher and a student in your relationship means being open to learning and teaching.

Sometimes I'm the one who needs guidance, and other times I can provide insight. But I've found that a brilliant relationship involves both partners educating each other on things big and small. This means being open to new perspectives, challenging each other in positive ways, and accepting that we're never done learning.

Being the student means I'm always willing to listen and grow, and being the teacher means I have something valuable to share that can help my partner become the best version of themselves. This dynamic is what creates emotional depth and real intimacy.

6. Be a Protector and Provider

This is something that's often misunderstood. Being a protector and provider doesn't just mean providing financially or physically protecting my partner. It means being the *emotional anchor*, the person who keeps the peace and ensures that the relationship is a safe space for growth. I've learned that being a protector isn't about controlling or micromanaging. It's about offering emotional stability, being present when things are tough, and stepping up when needed. It's about providing support, whether that's through tough decisions, tough days, or simply being a shoulder to lean on.

Being a provider also means creating a safe, nurturing environment where my partner can be their true self, free from fear or judgment.

7. Think Outside the Box and Maintain Self-Control

A brilliant relationship isn't always about doing things the way everyone else does them. Sometimes, you have to think outside the box. Don't be afraid to innovate or try new things together. Relationships should evolve, not stay stagnant. The more creative you get with how you spend time together, solve problems, or communicate, the more interesting and fulfilling the relationship becomes.

Maintaining self-control is key. Relationships can trigger a lot of emotions—anger, frustration, jealousy—but I've learned that the best way to deal with these feelings is not to react impulsively. Taking a step back, breathing, and responding thoughtfully keeps things from escalating. Self-control is the ultimate form of respect for both myself and my partner.

8. Have a Great Sense of Humor

Finally, laughter is one of the greatest tools in any successful relationship. Having a good sense of humor means you don't take things too seriously. Life is filled with challenges, but when you can laugh together, you strengthen your bond. A shared sense of humor has been one of the things that's helped me navigate the ups and downs in my relationships. It's a reminder that no matter how serious things get, there's always room for joy and playfulness. Life is too short to be angry or upset all the time. A little laughter goes a long way in making every moment, even the difficult ones, more bearable.

These eight principles—wisdom, listening, communication, actions, teaching and learning, protection, self-control, and humor—are the ingredients for a brilliant relationship. I know that if I can embody these practices consistently, I'll create a relationship that's grounded in respect, love, and mutual growth.

FOUNDATIONS OF A HEALTHY RELATIONSHIP

Healthy relationships don't just happen by accident. They aren't built on fleeting passion, convenience, or luck. So far, we have learned that real, lasting relationships require conscious effort, patience, and a willingness to grow together. It's easy to get caught up in the excitement of a new relationship, but without a solid foundation, things can crumble when life inevitably throws challenges our way. Through experience, observation, and hard lessons, I've identified some key components that help build a relationship that not only survives but thrives. These are principles that I try to live by—practices that keep a relationship fulfilling, secure, and emotionally rich.

1. Understand Your Partner: One of the biggest mistakes I've made in past relationships was assuming I already knew everything about my partner. But understanding someone isn't a one-time achievement; it's a continuous process. Every person has layers—emotions, triggers, dreams, and fears—and these evolve over time. A healthy relationship requires me to actively learn about my partner, not just in the early honeymoon phase, but always. Understanding my partner means:

    - Paying attention to their needs, even when unspoken.

- Learning their love language—what makes them feel most valued?
- Recognizing their emotional triggers and avoiding unnecessary conflicts.
- Supporting their dreams, even if they are different from mine.

The moment I stop seeking to understand, I start taking my partner for granted. And that's the beginning of a disconnection.

2. Be a Good Listener: This one took time for me to master. As men, we're often programmed to fix problems. When my partner talks about her struggles, my instinct used to be: "Here's how you fix it." But I've come to realize that sometimes, she doesn't want solutions—she just wants to be heard. Being a good listener means:
    - Not interrupting when my partner speaks.
    - Validating their feelings, even if I don't fully relate.
    - Listening without forming my response while they're still talking.
    - Asking follow-up questions to show genuine interest.

3. Respect Each Other's Boundaries: Respect is one of the most underrated elements of a strong relationship. It's easy to assume that love alone is enough, but without respect, love turns into control, resentment, or suffocation. Boundaries keep

a relationship healthy because they allow both partners to maintain individuality while growing together. Respecting boundaries means:

- Acknowledging that my partner needs space sometimes, and so do I.
- Avoiding invasive questions or forcing them to share things they're not ready to.
- Not controlling their decisions, friendships, or personal time.
- Recognizing that "no" means "no," even in small matters.

4. Give Sincere Compliments: It's easy to assume that once I've won my partner over, I don't need to keep reminding her how amazing she is. But appreciation shouldn't stop once the chase is over. I've made it a habit to give my partner sincere compliments—not just on her looks, but on her mind, her effort, her kindness, and her strength. Women notice the little things, and genuine words of appreciation reinforce love and security.

5. Don't Let Emotions Dictate Your Words: I've had moments where my emotions got the best of me—where anger or frustration made me say things I later regretted. I've learned that in a relationship, words hold power. They can build or destroy, heal or wound. The best advice I ever received? Never

say something in anger that you wouldn't want to be the last thing your partner remembers you saying. Thinking before I speak means:

- Taking a deep breath before reacting.
- Asking myself, "Will this help the situation, or make it worse?"
- Choosing words that express how I feel without attacking my partner.

6. Practice Patience and Compromise: No two people will ever see eye to eye on everything. But I've realized that stubbornness is the enemy of growth. A relationship isn't about winning arguments—it's about understanding each other. Practicing patience and compromise means:
    - Letting go of the need to always be right.
    - Meeting in the middle, even when it's inconvenient.
    - Accepting that love requires small sacrifices every day.

7. Hold a Positive, Mandatory Progress Meeting Every 3 Months: I started doing this in my relationships, and it changed everything. Every few months, we sit down and talk—not about bills, work, or daily routines, but about us. This isn't about pointing fingers. It's about making sure we're on the same page and growing together. A relationship check-in means:
    - Discussing what's working and what's not.

- Bringing up small concerns before they turn into big problems.
- Setting goals for the next few months—emotionally, financially, and personally.

8. Sacrifice for Each Other: I'll say this again, love isn't about keeping score. I've learned that small sacrifices—choosing my partner's happiness over my temporary comfort—go a long way. A healthy relationship is one where both partners feel like they have a teammate for life. Sacrifice here means:
    - Supporting their dreams, even when they require adjustments.
    - Showing up when they needs you, even if you're tired or busy.
    - Defending them in public and correcting them in private, with love.

9. Try New Things Together: Routine can kill passion. That's why I make it a point to introduce new experiences into the relationship. Whether it's trying a new hobby, traveling to an unfamiliar place, or learning something together, novelty keeps the connection fresh. Trying new things also means:
    - Finding shared passions to strengthen your bond.
    - Avoiding complacency—continuously dating each other.
    - Keeping intimacy exciting and spontaneous.

10. Keep Outside Distractions in Check: One of the biggest relationship killers? External influences. Whether it's negative friends, toxic family members, or social media distractions, outside noise can create unnecessary tension. Protecting your relationship means:
    - Prioritizing my partner's feelings over outsiders' opinions.
    - Keeping personal issues private.
    - Recognizing when someone else's negativity is affecting our peace.

At the core, I've come to understand that relationships aren't just about how much we love each other, but about how well we treat each other. By following these principles, I know I can build a relationship that is strong, fulfilling, and truly built to last.

CONCLUSION

Relationships are among the most rewarding yet challenging experiences we navigate in life. They hold the potential for immense joy, deep companionship, and personal growth—but they can also be the source of heartbreak, disappointment, and disillusionment. Throughout this book, we've explored the illusions that often distort our understanding of love, exposing the falsehoods that lead to unrealistic expectations, toxic behaviors, and emotional suffering.

But in the midst of these challenges, there is also hope. True love, the kind that endures, is not built on illusions but on a foundation of honesty, vulnerability, and mutual respect. It requires effort, self-awareness, and the willingness to see both ourselves and our partners for who we truly are—not as projections of what we wish they would be.

We've examined the deception, selfishness, and manipulation that can turn relationships into battlegrounds. But we have also uncovered the antidotes: the courage to be honest, the power of vulnerability, and the strength that comes from setting and respecting boundaries. Love flourishes not when we cling to fantasies, but when we embrace reality—choosing to understand rather than control, to listen rather than assume, and to nurture rather than demand.

The struggles we've discussed are not unique to any one person. They are reflections of larger societal issues—how we are taught to view love, what we expect from relationships, and the emotional baggage we carry from past experiences. That said, if we want to build something real, something lasting, we must first do the work within ourselves. Healing is essential. Self-reflection is non-negotiable. And above all, honesty is important—both with ourselves and with those we invite into our hearts.

Love is not about perfection. It is not about control. It is about partnership—a commitment to growth, trust, and unwavering support. The choices we make today determine the relationships we build tomorrow. If we want love that is fulfilling, secure, and genuine, then we must choose with intention. Choose honesty over comfort. Choose respect over ego. Choose love that is real, not love that is convenient.

At the end of the day, the relationships we cultivate become the foundation for the lives we lead. And when that foundation is built on truth, understanding, and mutual care, it becomes unbreakable—standing the test of time, challenges, and change.

So, as you move forward, take what you've learned, reflect on your own patterns, and make the conscious decision to love with open eyes. Because love, when built the right way, is not just a fleeting emotion—it is a legacy that shapes who we are and the life we create.

www.ingramcontent.com/pod-product-compliance
Lightning Source LLC
LaVergne TN
LVHW022009200926
848481LV00007B/2301